Well-behaved women seldom make history.
—LAUREL THATCHER ULRICH

Dolley Madison

KATHLEEN KRULL

interior illustrations by
Steve Johnson and Lou Fancher

BLOOMSBURY
NEW YORK   LONDON   NEW DELHI   SYDNEY

To Dr. Helen Foster James,
a woman who breaks the rules

Text copyright © 2015 by Kathleen Krull
Interior illustrations copyright © 2015 by Steve Johnson and Lou Fancher
Cover illustration © 2015 by Edwin Fotheringham

First published in the United States of America in June 2015
by Bloomsbury Children's Books
www.bloomsbury.com

Bloomsbury is a registered trademark of Bloomsbury Publishing Plc

For information about permission to reproduce selections from this book, write to
Permissions, Bloomsbury Children's Books, 1385 Broadway, New York, New York 10018
Bloomsbury books may be purchased for business or promotional use. For information on bulk purchases please contact
Macmillan Corporate and Premium Sales Department at specialmarkets@macmillan.com

Library of Congress Cataloging-in-Publication Data
Krull, Kathleen.
Women who broke the rules : Dolley Madison / by Kathleen Krull ; illustrated by Steve Johnson and Lou Fancher.
pages   cm
Includes bibliographical references.
ISBN 978-0-8027-3794-6 (paperback) • ISBN 978-0-8027-3793-9 (hardcover)
1. Madison, Dolley, 1768–1849—Juvenile literature. 2. Presidents' spouses—United States—Biography—Juvenile literature.
I. Johnson, Steve, illustrator. II. Fancher, Lou, illustrator. III. Title. IV. Title: Dolley Madison.
E342.1.K78 2015   973.5'1092—dc23   [B]   2014009920

Art created with acrylic on watercolor paper
Typeset in Beaufort
Book design by Nicole Gastonguay

Printed in China by Leo Paper Products, Heshan, Guangdong
2 4 6 8 10 9 7 5 3 1 (paperback)
2 4 6 8 10 9 7 5 3 1 (hardcover)

All papers used by Bloomsbury Publishing, Inc., are natural, recyclable products
made from wood grown in well-managed forests. The manufacturing processes
conform to the environmental regulations of the country of origin.

TABLE OF CONTENTS

1 · THREE SECRET WEAPONS

D olley Payne was born with extra zip. And she was going
to need as much energy as she could muster.

All the rules in the new country of America were stacked
against women. They were like property, first belonging to
their fathers, then their husbands. They couldn't attend col-
lege. No respectable jobs were open to them. They couldn't
vote or have any role in government. In fact, America's FF
(Founding Fathers) believed women in politics would be
unnatural—"the world turned upside down."

Dolley was born in a log cabin on May 20, 1768. She was the third of eight children. And, yes, Dolley was her real name—not Dolly, Dorothy, or Dorothea.

Her relatives had come to America like so many others—in search of better lives and religious freedom. On her mother's side, they were Quakers, or members of the Society of Friends. Her father, after their marriage, applied to be a Quaker too.

Being a Quaker was important to Dolley's family. They were living in the New Garden Quaker settlement in North Carolina. But when Dolley was one year old, for reasons never clear, her father uprooted the family. They moved from farm to farm in eastern Virginia.

The Quaker religion wasn't for everybody. Quakers did not believe in fighting in a war, owning human beings (slavery), dancing, playing cards, or wearing flashy clothes or jewelry. You could even get thrown right out of the Quakers. Anyone who failed at his business or married outside the faith to a "stranger" could be "read out" at a meeting, or disowned.

Later, Dolley complained about the way Quaker rules "used to control me entirely." She tried to conform, wearing her plain gray dresses and modest caps. But she ached to rebel. Her grandmother may have helped her, sometimes letting her wear nicer clothes. Some frowned upon Dolley for being too "dashing," attracting too much attention.

But Dolley had secret weapons that helped her, and one of them was a Quaker rule. Unlike most people at the time, Quakers believed that men and women should have equal education. That's why Dolley could read and write much better than the average American.

When she was fifteen, her father uprooted the family again. Running a farm in Virginia depended on slave labor. As a good Quaker, he had wanted to free his slaves, but Virginia law wouldn't let him. As soon as the law changed, he let the slaves go and moved his family to the city—Philadelphia, Pennsylvania. This was then the capital of the United States, home to its Congress, and also a Quaker headquarters.

It was a tense time for Dolley. Her father tried to go into business as a merchant, selling starch for laundries. He failed. He was promptly "read out" at a Quaker meeting. Humiliated at being disowned, he took to his bed.

But Dolley had a second secret weapon: a strong mother.

Dolley's mom opened a boarding house for officials traveling to Congress, which was right around the corner. With Dolley helping, the house became very successful. It was here that Dolley learned how to hold her own around powerful men.

But even from his bed, her father controlled her life. For example, he picked her husband and she had no say. All her life, conflict upset her, and she wouldn't have been likely to argue.

At twenty-two she married her father's choice—a young Quaker lawyer named John Todd. Luckily, she liked him. They had two children and lived comfortably in Philadelphia.

Then the deadly yellow fever reached town in 1793. Spread by mosquitoes, the horrible disease killed one of every five people in Philadelphia. The victims, alas, included Dolley's new baby and her husband.

Now she was a widow with a one-year-old son, Payne, to support. At twenty-five Dolley was starting over. Good thing she had a third secret weapon working for her.

That extra zip.

One day, a few months after John's death, a senator in Congress sent a message to Dolley. A very important American would like to meet her—for a date.

She wrote to her best friend that "the great little Madison has asked . . . to see me this evening."

James Madison really was little. At five feet four inches, he was two inches shorter than Dolley, so slight that he often faded into the background. He was also seventeen years older than she was. He was going bald, powdering his remaining hair and pulling it back with a black ribbon. He always wore black clothes, as if life were a funeral. He spoke in low tones and tended to stand with his hands behind him. Not a good first impression.

But he was also really great. His was possibly the most brilliant mind in America. And he put it to work, helping to build his new country. In fact, James was such a key FF that he was known as the "Father of the Constitution." He also had a cool best friend—Thomas Jefferson, a fellow FF who was about to become the third president.

James Madison was rich, gentle, fond of Dolley's son, Payne, and, after a few more dates, madly in love with Dolley. Was she madly in love with him? Perhaps not at first. She did take the summer off to consider his marriage proposal. But in her world, she was no one without a husband, and she made the bold, brave decision to say yes.

At their wedding on September 15, 1794, she wore a ring and necklace James had given her. How delicious to wear jewelry for the first time! She was saying good-bye to her Quaker days. In fact, because James was Episcopalian, the Quakers promptly read her out for marrying someone outside the faith. But this didn't bother her family, and all her life she remained close to her mother and sisters.

Marrying James was the best decision Dolley ever made. He was the secret weapon that gave her a full life and put her on the national stage.

"Our hearts understand each other," she told him later.

Their forty-one-year marriage was truly loving. Neither could stand conflict, so they rarely argued. They hated being apart and when they were, they wrote each other mushy letters twice a day. In private they teased and played like children. She called him "little Jemmy" and sometimes even hoisted him on her back to prove that she was stronger.

James tried to be a good stepfather to her son. But both parents avoided conflict so much, even with Payne, that the boy became spoiled. Dolley could never say no to him.

They lived at Montpelier, the lavish Madison estate in

Orange, Virginia. It was filled with Persian carpets and lots of art and sculptures with American themes. To Dolley it was heavenly. The two thousand acres of its plantation were divided into four farms. Each included cabins for slaves who had all the skills needed to keep Montpelier running.

James hated slavery. He saw clearly how it clashed with the new democratic ideals. Still, he continued to have some sixty slaves, more or less, depending on how well the plantation was doing each year. Along with her plain clothes, Dolley apparently shed her Quaker antislavery beliefs.

The Madisons' social life was buzzy, including frequent visits to see Jefferson at his nearby estate, Monticello. Dolley's peppy ways charmed everyone. As one of her nieces put it, "You like yourself more when you are with her."

After Madison, Dolley's second-biggest fan was Jefferson. No one hated women in the public eye more than Jefferson—he called them "too wise to wrinkle their foreheads with politics." But Dolley's skill at getting along with people was unique, and he adored her.

In 1801 their pal Jefferson was sworn in as the third US president. The capital, meanwhile, had moved from Philadelphia to Washington in the new District of Columbia. Washington, DC, started out as a village.

Jefferson chose Madison as his secretary of state, and asked Dolley for a favor. His wife had died years earlier, but Jefferson felt that certain events, to be proper, needed a woman to cohost. Would Dolley come to the president's house—gradually becoming known as the White House—and help?

Would she! Dolley jumped in with her usual zest. Over the next eight years, she became known as a bubbly White House hostess. Her smile was warm as she welcomed everyone—political enemies as well as friends, ambassadors from other countries, and chiefs from various Indian nations.

Jefferson was able to double the size of America by buying the uncharted Louisiana Territory from France. Dolley helped out by raising the money to support the Lewis and Clark Expedition that explored it.

All the while, Dolley was also helping James, so shy in public. Thanks to her, more and more people were clueing in to his brilliance. The office of secretary of state became more powerful than it had been. Most now saw Madison as the natural president to follow Jefferson.

Dolley, it turned out, was even more of a secret weapon for James than he was for her.

3 "EVERYBODY LOVES MRS. MADISON"

During James's presidential campaign, Dolley acted as his unofficial manager. Naturally, he won.

He was sworn in as the country's fourth president in 1809. His voice trembled too much for people to hear him, and he looked pale—"scarcely able to stand," said a witness. At the ball afterward, James was heard to murmur, "I would rather be home in bed."

But Dolley positively bloomed. So many people crowded around her at the ball that a few fainted. Windows were broken on purpose to let in air.

Many wives of presidents have felt that they've been prisoners. Not Dolley. She *loved* her new role, and got to work.

America was still very new, very fragile. Some feared that it could still fall apart, or fall to its enemy, Great Britain. Even the location of the capital was a cause for worry. Washington was like a giant construction site, mostly swamp, with muddy paths instead of roads. Conditions were so bad that few women joined their husbands there at first. Some felt the capital should be moved back to Philadelphia, or to any other city.

Dolley didn't waste time complaining.

Two months after moving into the White House, she began a tradition of "Mrs. Madison's Wednesday nights." Anyone could come and talk to her and her husband. Soon this was *the* place to be seen. The events came to be known as squeezes because two to three hundred people were showing up, muddy feet and all. "The more she has round her, the happier she appears to be," said a guest.

These were nothing like the stuffy events of past presidents. These were fizzy and fun, with music and laughter and yummy food. But they also served a purpose. The squeezes were a way for people to share news and gossip, make connections, and gain more confidence in their country.

One of Dolley's many strengths was never forgetting a name or face. One night a man was so nervous when she called him by name that he spilled his coffee. Totally flustered, he tried to stuff the cup into his pocket. Dolley simply called for more coffee and started praising the man's "excellent mother" until he completely relaxed.

Very huggy, she called women "honey." And women were more than welcome at the squeezes. This was a time when enemies thought nothing of settling their differences with fistfights and duels. But the presence of Dolley and other women softened the rough edges.

If she heard an argument between men getting too tense, she would have punch and cake sent over to them. She often carried a novel so she could have something to chat about. Always her goal was unity, having people get along.

Dolley Madison, in her glory, was doing more than just about anyone to establish Washington, DC, as a real capital city, equal to the capitals in Europe.

She even used clothes to help. She befriended the wife of the French minister, who introduced her to French fashion. Now she was leaving her Quaker days far, far behind.

She wore the finest dresses and always something new—satin gowns embroidered with butterflies (no two alike), or dresses trimmed with fur or made of fabric that changed color in the light.

Stylish turbans were her trademark, and into them she stuck bird-of-paradise feathers from Paris or ostrich feathers. With her plumes, you could always spot her in a room (plus now she really towered over James). Her outfits dazzled people and made her seem powerful.

Dolley herself was becoming a tourist attraction, a bit like a rock star in her fame. Many women adopted her as their role model. She lacked an official title, but some called her the "Presidentess."

"Everybody loves Mrs. Madison," raved a senator, to which she shot right back, "That's because Mrs. Madison loves everybody."

4 ROLLING UP HER SLEEVES

Dolley was always finding ways to roll up her fancy sleeves to help James and the country.

In her dark green carriage, she made a point of visiting every new representative or senator. These visits took more of her time as the nation and the number of congressmen grew.

While James met with the men in his cabinet, she hosted "dove parties" for their wives. Sometimes she took groups of women to view sessions in Congress and the Supreme

Court. Always she kept her ears open for information to pass on to her husband, especially once the threat of war with Great Britain loomed.

She raised money to help the poor and to increase literacy, inspiring other women to follow her example.

She hosted tasty dinner parties, more than any other president's wife in history. In a slightly shocking move, she often sat at the head of the table and led the conversation so James didn't have to. Her table became "America's table,"

a showcase for local foods. She scored points by asking other political wives for their recipes. Only the finest wines and the fanciest of desserts, like the newfangled pink peppermint ice cream, were served.

Whenever James's male secretary was sick, Dolley filled in, taking dictation and doing business. If James was too ill to work, she might take on some of his duties. Theirs was an unusual partnership for the time.

Yet she was careful to be seen *not* as a partner but as

James's student. "You know I am not much of a politician," she would plead while giving her opinion.

Dolley wasn't just a people pleaser; she was increasingly informed. She didn't take public stands. Yet she always kept up with the news by letter, newspapers, and visitors' gossip. She attended any hearings and sessions that were open to the public.

She had a blast with her role—she loved to meddle, play matchmaker, offer advice, and foster the careers of the young men she approved of.

Did everyone like Dolley?

No, some thought she was *too* charming, acted too much like a queen, or was just too *much*. When she showed off America's bounty, some thought her meals too lavish, like platters for farmers instead of elegant banquets. She sometimes gambled and played cards, thought of as "common" activities by some.

Her colorful pet macaw, Polly, inspired a national fad for parrots, but Polly could also be very annoying. She screeched mostly in French, her language laced with swear words, and sometimes she scared people by dive-bombing. Once, when the president was defending a visitor from her, she bit James's finger down to the bone.

Still, most admired Dolley hugely—even more after she took on the job of remodeling the White House. Jefferson had totally neglected it during his eight years in office, and it was growing simply shabby with all of the Madisons' visitors and squeezes. Congress whipped up a budget of twenty thousand dollars for repairs.

Typically, the job would have been a man's responsibility. But it was Dolley who rose to the challenge—with flair. Working with a noted architect, she chose new wallpaper, furniture, red velvet drapes, and china.

Whenever possible, she bought American goods. She wanted people to think of the White House as their national home. She bought a precious piano, a guitar, a chess set, and formal portraits of George Washington and other notable American figures.

Actually, that portrait of Washington led to one of the Madisons' few spats. Where should they hang it? Dolley wanted it in her new Oval Room; James wanted it in the dining room. She was the one to back down. The life-size painting went on display where James had wanted it, hung in such a heavy frame that it had to be nailed to the dining room wall.

Not only did she remake the White House from top to

bottom, she came in under budget at $12,669.31. The new White House sparkled—it was worthy of a great nation.

But the old country, Great Britain, wasn't impressed with the new country, much less its seat of power. The British were firing on American ships, aiding Indian tribes in fighting against white settlers, and finding lots of other ways to show disrespect. As tensions rose, it was more important than ever to keep Americans informed, calm, and unified. One tool was Dolley's squeezes, which were moved into one of the prettiest rooms in America—the Oval Room, with its drapes of red velvet—in 1810.

The Madisons may not have liked to fight, but America couldn't find a way to keep the peace. After more and more insults from Great Britain, the United States declared war on June 18, 1812.

The War of 1812 is sometimes called the Second War of Independence. It was all about issues left over from the Revolutionary War. Mainly, Britain wanted a do-over.

Those who disapproved of the conflict called it "Mr. Madison's War" and were horrified when the British won the early battles. It wasn't at all certain that the young country would survive.

So Dolley waged her own war, winning people over with more parties, more music, and better treats. Now as many as five hundred guests came to the squeezes. "My head is *dizzy*!" she admitted. She'd invite troops in for snacks and reassure everyone that James had the situation under control.

This wasn't strictly true. By 1814 some four thousand well-armed British soldiers were said to be heading straight to Washington.

People began fleeing the city in panic. They left black clouds of dust in their trail. But not Dolley. James had to go inspect his troops in Maryland. He worried about his wife, warning her to be ready to leave at a moment's notice. "I am not afraid of anything," she wrote to him. But she started sleeping with a sword by her bed, just in case.

On August 24, she was planning a dinner party for forty to comfort people still in the city. The mayor came twice to ask her to leave. Dolley was determined to wait for James.

Finally, at three o'clock that afternoon, she heard the roar of approaching cannons. "Mr. Madison comes not," she fretted. But the enemy was here. It was time to go.

From her table in the dining room, she noticed that portrait of George Washington. It seemed a symbol of all America stood for. Suddenly she couldn't stand the thought

of leaving without it. Dolley was seized with fear that British troops would parade it through London's streets in triumph and ridicule.

Yet the huge painting's frame was still nailed to the wall and would not be easy to remove. Dolley gave orders to break the heavy frame and carefully cut George out of it. Then she sent the canvas to safety in a nearby barn.

Dolley took off right behind the portrait, only hours before the invading troops arrived.

As the sun was setting, the British marched into Washington, gleefully torching buildings as they went. They headed to the White House for the ultimate prize—taking James and his wife prisoner.

But no one was home. How annoying. The British admiral had to settle for stealing Dolley's red velvet seat cushion.

The admiral's troops had a fine time sitting down to enjoy the food and wines she had planned on serving at dinner.

After the meal, they set the entire White House on fire.

Safe on a plantation ten miles away, Dolley watched the flames against the black sky. She couldn't believe it. Except for Washington's portrait, all she had contributed to the White House—the piano, the fine furniture, and the decorations—turned to ashes. It wasn't just her loss; America had lost its home too. She was unable to speak of that night without crying. "My whole heart mourned for my country!" she said.

On the second day of the British invasion, a freak thunderstorm doused much of the fire. The winds and rain were so severe that the admiral ordered his troops to get out of Washington.

Two days later she and James returned to see the black shell of the house. Though rebuilding began quickly, the Madisons never again lived there, and stayed in private houses nearby.

Word spread about Dolley's heroic rescue of George. Now she wasn't just a great hostess but a national heroine.

Had the British gone on to win the war, it would have meant the end of the United States. But American troops finally crushed the enemy at the Battle of New Orleans in 1815. The war ended with both countries signing a peace treaty. Britain was *never* going to take their "colonies" back.

When the treaty arrived in Washington, Dolley celebrated with—what else?—a giant party.

The victory of the War of 1812 brought Americans together and made the country more stable—and Dolley was there every step of the way. Washington, DC, was more of a power center than ever.

When troops marched past her house, yelling three cheers in her honor, she would come outside and wave.

By 1817 it was James Monroe's turn to be president. Time for the Madisons to move along. But everyone hated to see them go. Mrs. Madison's Wednesday nights, or squeezes,

had lasted for all eight years of the Madison presidency. They had won her countless friends.

The couple stayed for a month after Monroe's election to attend all the parties in their honor. They finally left by steamboat in April 1817, then took a carriage to Montpelier.

James never went back to Washington again. Dolley was still only forty-eight, as peppy and interested in the world as ever. Her next nineteen years with James were happy, but part of her missed the buzz of Washington. She called herself a "poor dull creature" who was "withering" away.

Yet even at Montpelier, she was still the hostess with the mostest. She planned luscious dinners starting at four p.m. and lasting for hours. The dinners gave James a chance to tell stories about his accomplishments. "It was living history!" raved a guest.

The Madisons never had children together, but she was a world-class aunt to James's thirty nieces and nephews, plus her own young relatives. Dolley's son, Payne, continued to disappoint, doing little beyond running up huge gambling debts. He was even in prison several times for debt. Extremely embarrassing. But Payne was always Dolley's blind spot. She never stopped taking care of him.

Beside paying off Payne's debts, the Madisons had other money woes. Their crops had bad seasons, and they had a habit of living beyond their means. James had to sell off precious pieces of Montpelier to pay their bills.

As he aged, he couldn't stand to be apart from Dolley, and she took good care of him, his papers, and his legacy.

James died in 1836, when he was eighty-five and she was sixty-eight.

Dolley felt her heart break. But she pulled herself together and returned to Washington the following year. The social whirl welcomed her back, and she carried on for another thirteen glamorous years.

She continued to have money problems. Eventually she had no choice but to sell Montpelier.

As Dolley neared her eighties, people began having parties for *her*. This marvelous woman had known all twelve American presidents. As one senator put it, she was "the only permanent power in Washington." People loved that she'd used her social skills to help build a nation. She was especially beloved for saving that George Washington painting.

Honors piled up. She was the only person to be awarded an honorary seat in Congress, so she could watch debates. She was granted a lifetime of free postage at a time when mailing letters was costly.

Dolley died on July 12, 1849, in Washington, DC. At age eighty-one, she'd apparently suffered a stroke and died peacefully as she was surrounded by loving relatives.

Hers was the largest funeral ever held in the city at that time. It actually shut down the government—everyone wanted to attend.

During the service, President Zachary Taylor referred to Dolley as the "First Lady." This was a brand-new title. Dolley helped define the role of the First Lady, carving out a space for women on the national stage. All First Ladies since then have had her as a role model.

America's First Lady—how Dolley Madison would have loved it.

★ SOURCES AND FURTHER READING ★

Books
(* especially for young readers)

Allgor, Catherine. *A Perfect Union: Dolley Madison and the Creation of the American Nation.* New York: Henry Holt, 2007.

Chadwick, Bruce. *James and Dolley Madison: America's First Power Couple.* Amherst, NY: Prometheus Books, 2014.

* Fritz, Jean. *The Great Little Madison.* New York: Putnam, 1989.

* Grace, Catherine O. *The White House: An Illustrated History.* New York: Scholastic, 2003.

Hyland, Matthew G. *Montpelier and the Madisons: House, Home and American Heritage.* Charleston, SC: History Press, 2007.

Ketcham, Ralph. *The Madisons at Montpelier: Reflections on the Founding Couple.* Charlottesville: University of Virginia Press, 2009.

* Larkin, Tanya. *What Was Cooking in Dolley Madison's White House?* New York: Powerkids Press, 2001.

* Mayo, Edith P. *The Smithsonian Book of the First Ladies: Their Lives, Times, and Issues.* New York: Henry Holt, 1996.

O'Brien, Cormac. *Secret Lives of the First Ladies: What Your Teachers Never Told You About the Women of the White House.* Philadelphia: Quirk, 2005.

* Quackenbush, Robert M. *James Madison and Dolley Madison and Their Times.* New York: Pippin Press, 1992.

Shulman, Holly Cowan. *Dolley Madison: Her Life, Letters, and Legacy.* New York: Rosen Publishing, 2003.

Taylor, Elizabeth Dowling. *A Slave in the White House: Paul Jennings and the Madisons.* New York: Palgrave Macmillan, 2012.

Truman, Margaret. *First Ladies: An Intimate Group Portrait of White House Wives.* New York: Random House, 1995.

Websites

Dolley Madison, C-Span's "First Ladies: Influence and Image":
http://firstladies.c-span.org/FirstLady/5/Dolley-Madison.aspx

Dolley Madison, PBS's American Experience:
www.pbs.org/wgbh/americanexperience/films/dolley

The Dolley Madison Digital Edition: **http://rotunda.upress.virginia.edu/dmde**

The Dolley Madison Project: **www2.vcdh.virginia.edu/madison**

James Madison's Montpelier: **www.montpelier.org**

★ INDEX ★